Like a Murmur in the Wind

LINDA BALCOM FELLERS

ISBN 978-1-64028-002-1 (Paperback)
ISBN 978-1-64028-003-8 (Digital)

Christian Faith Publishing, Inc.
296 Chestnut Street
Meadville, PA 16335
www.christianfaithpublishing.com

Printed in the United States of America

The Book most Holy

Alone in the darkness
At the beginning of time
Man appeared here on Earth and
And committed a crime.

A price must be paid
For these teachings of old
Someone is responsible
Or so we are told.

Our Lord, Christ Jesus bowed his head
Taking upon himself, praying for the dead
His battered and bruised body
Was just the beginning
His grace and his crown
He gave to the living.

He died on the cross to save us our pain
Today or tomorrow, it is all the same
His message is clear, there is much to gain
His journey is told in the Book most Holy.

Alone in the darkness we are no more
The Light of forgiveness we do implore
The price we owed has been fully paid
By our Savior the son, now we are saved.

Looking in the rearview mirror is no way to live; yesterday is gone.

All will eventually have to learn to cope with pain and loss. As individuals, all will have a path to travel and all will be different. Some seek God's presence while others will shake their fist at Him. It is in the acceptance of life and death that inner peace will surface. Hold your memories close and take a step forward, one day at a time.

I am not aware of another book to compare with this one as this is a personal compilation of experiences that are mine alone. It is not about religion, but about death and life, personal growth, inner strength and struggle, and using what you have learned to be of help to others.

Life is indeed fleeting.

Disclaimer: I am not in the medical field nor associated with hospice. I am just called upon to be of service and spiritual enough to hear His urgings.

All photos and experiences are mine.

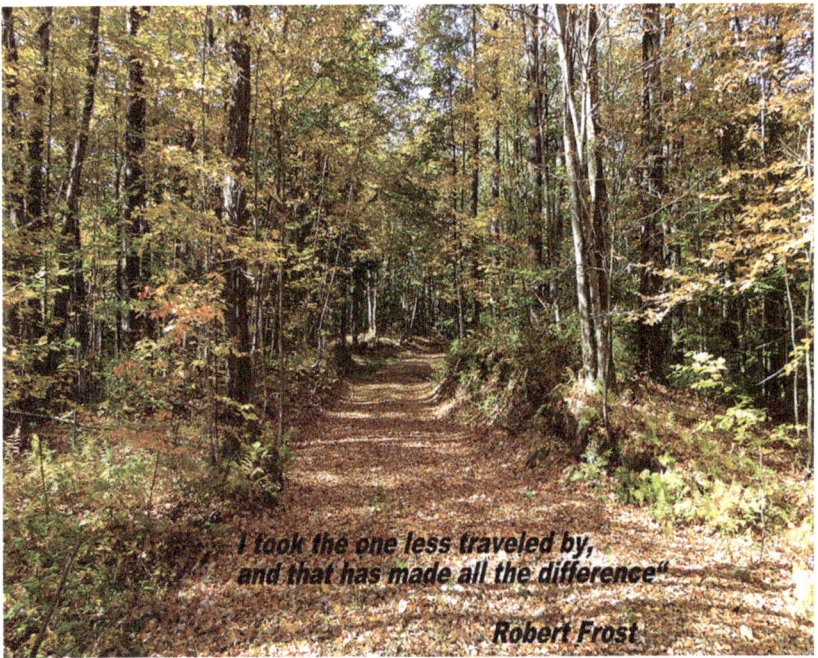

I took the one less traveled by,
and that has made all the difference"

Robert Frost

To tell my story completely would mean beginning where it started and building an outline of circumstances, experiences, and lessons learned along the way. Sometimes, God whispers in your ear like a murmur in the wind, and other times, it's like a blow to the head and heart with a "Can you hear me now?" I have come to realize through happenstance and repeated instances that I am in the place I need to be when I am most needed. One of my daughters calls me Deaths Angel, as I have literally been holding family members, friends, and even stranger's hands while helping them through prayer and quiet calmness to reach out and let go of this life with peace, dignity, and less fear of the unknown.

I will be the first person to tell you that I knew little about God and Jesus, except what I remembered from Sunday school as a child. I consider myself spiritual rather than deeply religious. I cannot walk in the woods or on the beach without seeing God's magnificence everywhere and being truly thankful.

I am quick to be thankful for everyday moments like catching that deer running through the woods or looking up and seeing double rainbows. I will admit, though, that I very rarely ask God for help for myself; in fact, I am extremely bad at this. It is important in all aspects of our lives to ask for help and be willing to give it also. Do what you can and ask for help; it gives others a purpose as well.

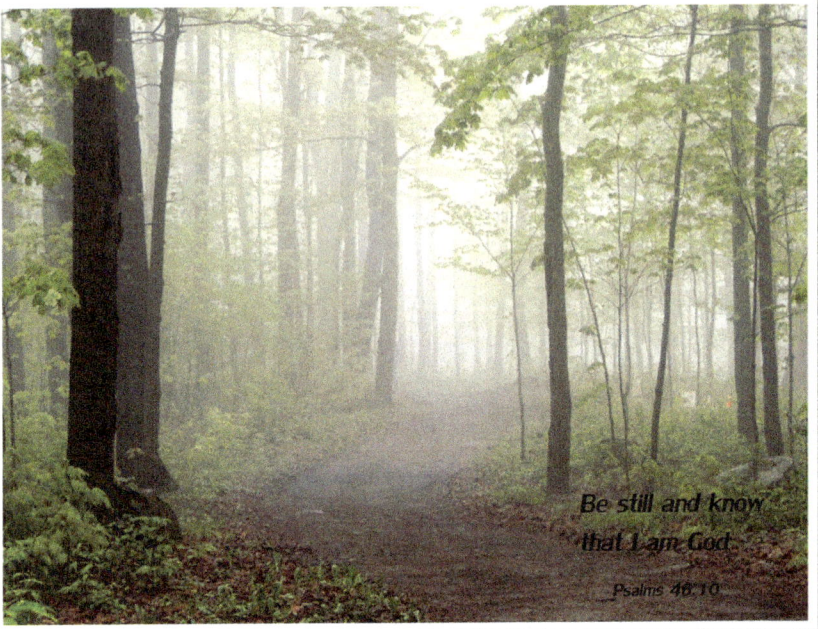

Be still and know that I am God.
Psalms 46:10

My grandfather has played an important role in both myself and my husband's life. He was a good man that loved his family without reservation. He was my husband's father figure, and we visited both my grandparents every weekend. When he was approaching his later years, he became very anxious and afraid of dying so much so that the time he should have been embracing life, he spent being scared. Death is a transition and is scary; none of us know for sure what lies ahead. If you have faith, it is easier for sure, but even then, it is human nature to want to cling to life.

After Grampa took ill, he was transported to the hospital. Family came and went. My parents had just left when my husband and I arrived. Soon, Grampa's legs began to hurt and so I thought massaging them may bring some relief, but it did not seem to make much difference. I later learned this was because the blood leaves the extremities to protect the heart, leaving the feet, legs, and touch points such as knees and fingers mottled and hurting. I rang for the nurse to see what was going on. My grandmother was in the waiting room as this was happening. She was hard of hearing and legally blind but got around very well. She came into his room, and I tried to tell her it was his time to go without being too loud as I was not sure if he could still hear and didn't want him to be afraid. I made sure she understood what was going on, and Grampa passed peacefully; neither alone nor scared.

Within this same time frame, my mother-in-law was also ill. She had been diagnosed with breast cancer that had metastasized and was at her home with hospice. This was my first experience with hospice. Their goal is to assist the family with care and function as liaisons with the doctors. I helped the best I could. I was not sure what to do and relied on the nurses for guidance. It was rough on the whole family, including her siblings, husband, and kids. She soon passed, but with a difficult and wholly different transition than I had witnessed with my Grampa. His death was a result of old age while hers was a disease. I helped the hospice nurse bathe her and put her in fresh pajamas. My hands were shaking, although I knew I couldn't hurt her, but I had never done this before. She was only sixty-two years old! This made me very angry to think that someone so young could be gone from our lives so quickly. I had yet to learn that it is all in God's time, not ours; this was my first step in realizing that the small stuff must fall by the wayside as inconsequential to my life or that of my family. We must pick our battles daily and not allow ourselves to get worked up over petty issues.

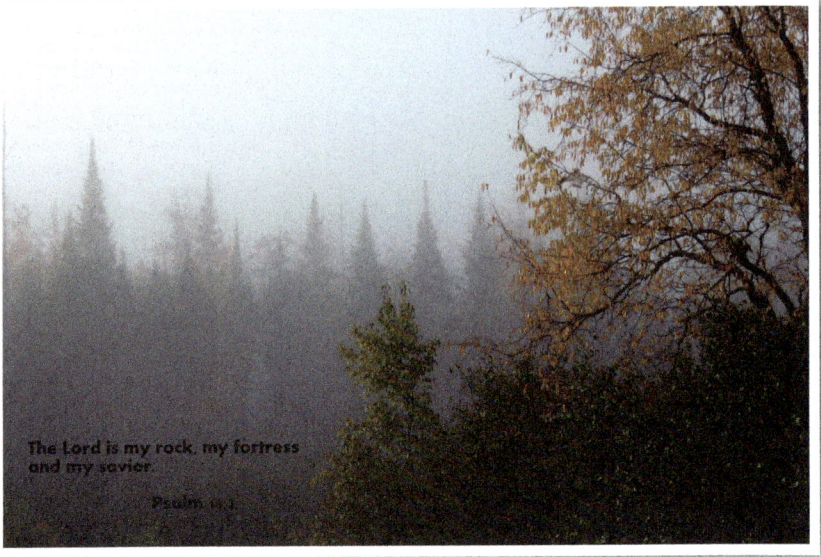

The Lord is my rock, my fortress and my savior.

Psalm 18:1

Time passed, and I had a few uneventful years but did eventually feel "His touch" upon me again in the form of an urging that help was needed. We had elderly neighbors with whom we were very close, to the extent that my children grew up calling them Grandma and Grandpa Baxter. Grandpa Baxter became very ill when his diabetes got out of control, and he could no longer leave his home. One day, he asked me to stay with him while his wife ran her errands. We were like family, and they were comfortable having me there. I did not hesitate, even though I had three young children at home. The kids were fine with my husband and I was needed elsewhere. At this point, I still did not realize God was working through me. I was developing humility and love for my fellow man, but when Grandpa Baxter died at home, I was more in survival mode, every death bringing me closer to understanding my personal place in this life.

I was with the Baxter's as part of their family, and it was very moving for me to be included in this private family time.

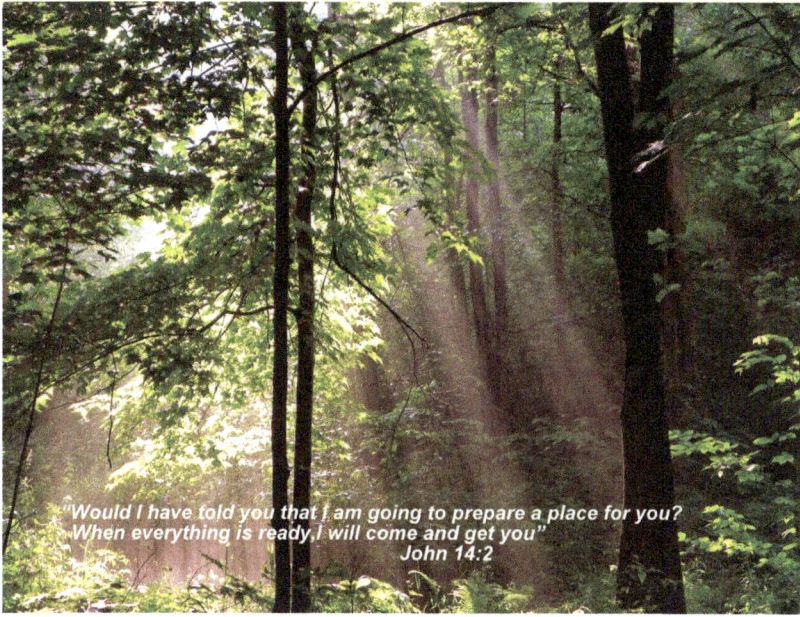

"Would I have told you that I am going to prepare a place for you?
When everything is ready, I will come and get you"
John 14:2

Nothing in my life could have prepared me for "the phone call" that changed my life forever. It was a direct hit to the heart. My parents' firstborn, David, who proceeded me by one and a half years, was particularly close to our parents. A retired Army veteran, he later became a Baptist minister and joined Dad in their own construction business. His wife and I have been friends since first grade, and I stood up with them at their wedding.

David's life was full—he performed the marriage ceremonies of both of his children and was just blessed with his first grandchild. That being said, I was truly horrified when he related to me one day that "if the Good Lord wants me, I am ready to go anytime." In retrospect, I now understand his thought process and his true belief in Christ Jesus. What was to happen next proved to be the catalyst upon which my spiritual growth quickly came into focus.

David was riding his motorcycle from his church and was within a half mile of his home when a truck pulled out of its lane in front of him to enter a driveway. It struck my brother, throwing him off the bike onto the side of the road. 911 was called, and they got him stabilized enough to get to a point where a helicopter could airlift him to the hospital. My parents, along with David's wife and kids, were notified and some of our siblings also met them at the hospital. My phone was temporarily out of order, so I did not know what was going on until my younger sister called. At first the doctors were optimistic as they knew he had a broken arm and took him into the OR to cast it. Very shortly, the doctor came out and gave our family the news that was so unexpected as to be unbelievable. He was gone! What... wait—shock, disbelief, horror, pain—no understanding of what was being said.

Apparently, when he was hit and thrown from the motorcycle, an artery was severed, but immediately clotted. To my understanding, this is a rarity. By the time he reached the OR, the clot released, and he was instantly gone. His wife gave permission to use his body to help others. He was only forty-four years old. It was at this time I truly turned to God for answers for the suddenness of his passing and the grief for our parents and his wife and children.

Looking back on it now, I can see I was needed here at home instead of at the hospital with my other family members. God knows what he's doing all the time. I called our younger brother who lives out of state and told him the events that had transpired and to come home. I then drove up to my eighty-year-old grandmother's and had to tell her that her oldest grandson had died. There really was no gentle way to deliver this kind of news to someone as frail as she was. It was and still is difficult to process as it all happened so quickly. Poor Grandma, she felt so sorry for her daughter (Mom).

When my parents got home, I was there waiting. Somehow, words came tumbling out of my mouth. I told them, "This is not the worst that could have happened." They were stunned at first. "What do you mean, he died!" I reminded them that he had said he was ready to go with his Lord. Well, it looks like he was ready, but we sure were not. I now stood front and center as oldest of the five remaining siblings, to take on my new role. David believed in his Lord, and that fact alone at that time in my life helped me get through the following weeks.

I gain much solace from walking the woods behind my house. The trees, the paths, the birds, and solitude all welcome me and expect nothing in return. I do this for myself, to center and ground myself in the moment. I find that solitude makes me stronger, and I prefer it when dealing with harsh realities.

I reach deep within for strength and accompanied my father to assist my sister-in-law with picking out my brother's casket. Who does this? I was to find as I kept moving forward that I do way more than I would like.

It was while on one of my nature walks that I kept asking "what do I do" over and over, so overwhelmed with grief. I could not comprehend my *brother* was gone. An inner voice I now believe was the Holy Spirit said, "Go back to the beginning," and I knew without hesitation it meant get out my Bible and read thy word. I would not say that religion at this point in my life was a factor in how I was living and would have had a hard time believing God would ever speak to me. This was the WHAM moment alluded to earlier and not merely a murmur in the wind.

After David's death, I heard him say to me, "Take care of Mom and Dad." He was passing his responsibility down to me. Upon hearing this, I will never doubt there is an afterlife.

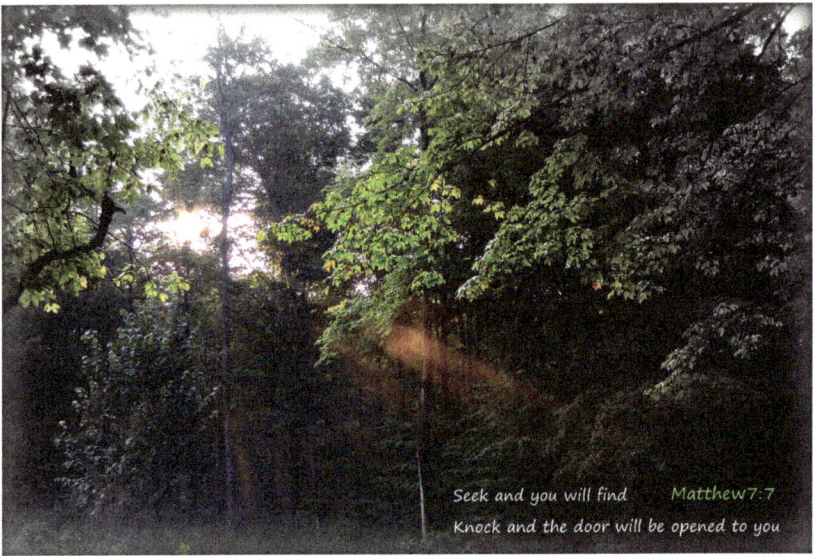

Seek and you will find   Matthew 7:7
Knock and the door will be opened to you

I proceed ahead another year. My grandmother is very sick, diagnosed with leukemia. My mom, my sisters, and myself are taking care of her at her home. I have found that as long as you are living, you are not dead yet! By this, I mean there is humor mixed in with the sadness and love with the fear. Grandma wanted this certain color nail polish and wanted me to order it for her. She loved fussing with her nails. I knew it would not arrive before she left us, so I told her it was back ordered and she was fine with that. A small fib for her peace of mind. She also wanted to get a nice tea cup and saucer for my mom for her birthday. I looked all over town and found one that I thought would do. She loved it, and at my suggestion, gave it to Mom early as her birthday wasn't for several weeks yet.

By this time, Grandma was in a hospital bed so we could adjust it for her comfort. She says to me one afternoon, "Linnie, climb up here with me." I looked at her and said, "Okay, but you will have to move over." She thought for a moment and replied "I can't!" We both started laughing and I did manage to grab an edge and climbed in, and we simply laid there talking. This quality time was just wonderful and I would have hated to have missed it. The next morning, she was gone, with us girls grouped around her. So many are alone. I cannot fathom passing without family or friends near.

About now you must be thinking, "Is death following her around?" It has crossed my mind, and I wonder myself why I am where I am and able to do what I do.

Remember my elderly neighbors, the Baxters? Well Grandma Baxter is close to ninety and has throat cancer, never having smoked a day in her life. How is this even fair? Guess what, folks, life is not fair. It isn't about me or how I feel; it was about helping her get through it. She was such an awesome inspiration, to be able to mow her own lawn and drive herself to town. A very strong pioneer woman. She had surgery and came home with a feeding tube; she was not a happy camper, but she adjusted for a period of time and even named that lifesaving nasty tube "Charlie"—how comical. Her spirits never revived, though, and she was just going through the motions to get through each day.

One morning, I went over for coffee and Grandma Baxters's daughter and granddaughters were there. She was baking bread and had the coffee going. She couldn't talk because of the cancer, so she motioned for me to make sure everyone was fed. That same afternoon, she retired to her bedroom and I could tell she was tired of the struggle. The family had a friend who was also a minister, and they called her in for prayer. I sat next to Grandma B and as I have learned to do, I silently talk to Jesus and ask him to release his child from her suffering and take her home. I have no specific reason why I do this silently, but I do and I can feel that I am evolving as Gods' will permits. I now believe in God; I believe Jesus walks in step with me, and I am positive of an afterlife.

At times, I wonder if what I gain in growth must be to the detriment of others. It is a human thought that I know not to be true; nevertheless, it passes through my mind and sometimes guilt sets in.

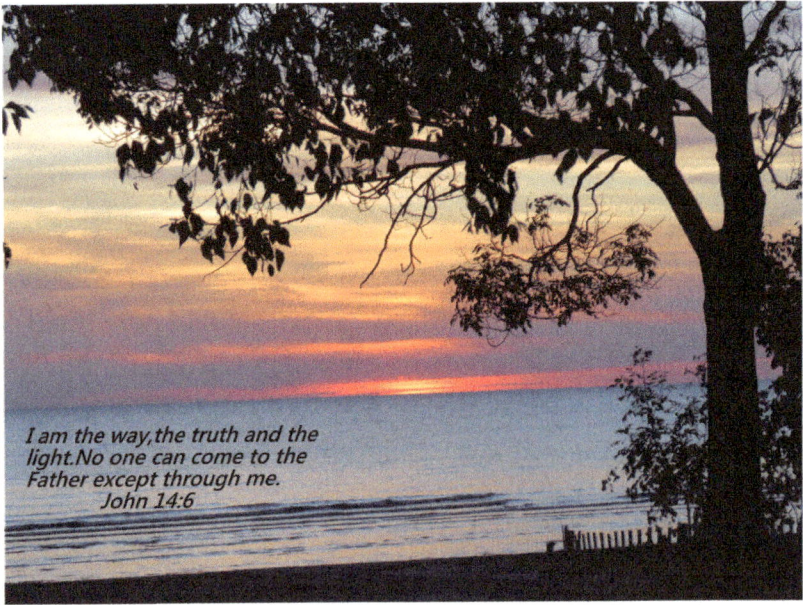

I am the way, the truth and the light. No one can come to the Father except through me.
John 14:6

Within weeks of Grandma Baxters's passing, I received a phone call from a stranger. I have no idea who she was or how she had gotten my name. She cried and pleaded with me to please come and stay the night as her companion was very ill with cancer and she desperately needed some sleep. I so did not want to do this and was trying to come up with some excuse. Knowing another death was imminent, I was scared and did not know what I would be walking into. My heart said go, and so I did. I gathered a few books, thinking to pass the time, and after I arrived, she went upstairs to sleep. Now I did not know the gentleman lying alone in his hospital bed but could see immediately that pity and prayer and help was needed in a big way. He was suffering from cancer with no nurses, no pain medication, nothing! It was horrible and inhumane. I did not read at all that night; rather, I sat and held his hand to keep him "grounded." By this, I mean a person needs human touch to keep oneself aware of one's surroundings. I prayed all night for this stranger. Being human, I also was a "clock watcher" as I wanted to go home, my safe place. This was a new experience for me, helping a person I had not met before, and such a helpless situation. A virtual stranger relying on another stranger. Come morning, he said thank-you and good-bye. His companion said it was the most peaceful night he'd had in a long time. He died later that same day. This day taught me humility and compassion for others. I never did know his name, but it does not matter. There was an immediate need that I hope I had a part in helping him to let go of the pain and step toward his Savior. Now this life event could very well have been to help this pleading woman, rather than the stranger in the bed. Makes you stop and think, doesn't it. There are many people involved in many situations. Who is to say whom is helping whom.

The sun rises at one end of the heavens and follows its course to the other end

Psalm 19:6

My dad, having smoked since he was a teenager, has developed lung cancer in his sixties. I truly think the loss of my brother brought so much pain to both my parents that it hurt to get through each day.

Dad had radiation treatments that seemed to help and he had a fairly good year, going for coffee with the guys, puttering around in his workshop. As the cancer progressed, it was not unusual for Mom to call and ask me to stay overnight. Dad wanted me there so she could get some sleep. He didn't rest much as the medications kept him awake a lot of the time. My parents usually slept in recliners at this point, and Dad would nudge Mom awake with his cane if he needed anything. When I stayed, she could go to her own bed.

There came a day when Dads' legs looked really swollen. As a family, we decided to take him to the hospital to see if they could do something about the situation. He was admitted and the lung doctor went into Dad's room to examine him. When he came back out, he advised us that Dad had a few hours left to live. What just happened? WHAM—oh, Lord, another shock to the system.

Once again, I called my brother and sister who lived out of state to come home. Dad was in quite a bit of pain and so I went to the nurses' station to request pain medication. One little shot of morphine and it worked, no more pain, but his body had had enough and he just slipped away. I honestly don't think he even knew he was leaving. Is this a good thing or would you want to know and say your good-byes? I don't know which is easier; I guess it depends on the individual.

I called my siblings back as they were on the road up, and trying not to say the actual words that Dad was gone, I told them there was no need to hurry, and they understood the message.

Before heading home, I went to the nurses' station and told them which funeral home to contact. Mom was just heading back from the elevators to do this, but I told her I had taken care of it. It needed doing, and I just did it thinking it was saving Mom from that particular task.

Right or wrong, when I am compelled by a need, I have learned to pay attention to my inner self and not worry about the consequences. I have rarely been steered wrong, and sometimes years later, when someone has commented, "Remember when you did this or said that?" I realize that actions impact others in ways you may never know at the time.

Even armed with knowledge and some confidence, this emotional roller coaster does a number on my emotions and physical health. I don't shout it out, but I am strong in my faith; otherwise, I would be a whimpering mass on the floor. This assurity allows me to make quick decisions and to live by the creed "There is always, always something to be thankful for."

You can't keep looking for the logic in an illogical situation. You need to totally forget the "touch or feel to be real" concept and go with your heart and instincts. I know I struggled for years to find reasons for God and Jesus. Give that up! It won't work. I was upset when my children were struggling with relationships and finances. I finally just asked Jesus to take it from me, and it was in his hands. There was such a revelation, a shiver literally went through me. Guess what? I finally got it right. What a glorious feeling not to be burdened with what I had no control over anyway. We need to live in the day, the moment even. It only comes once, and tomorrow will have its own set of issues.

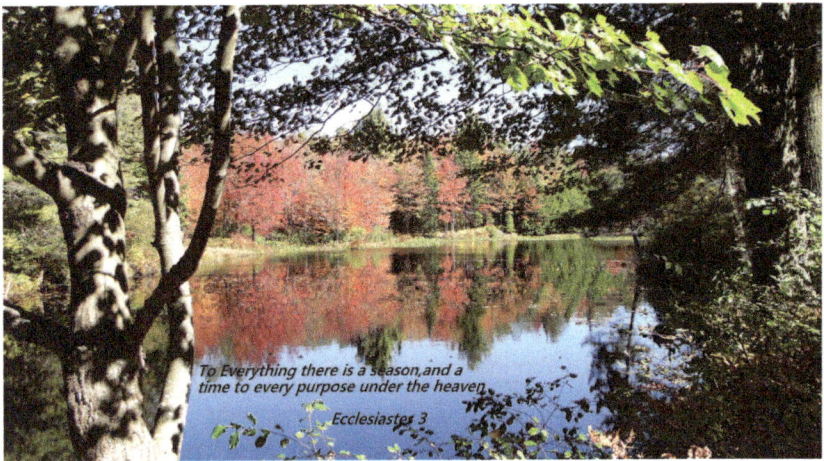

To Everything there is a season, and a time to every purpose under the heaven.
Ecclesiastes 3

This next part is even more personal and very hard for me to recount for you, but I must as it is part of the journey. My husband Roy of forty years was not feeling well and was misdiagnosed twice as having muscle spasms in his back. It took a second emergency room trip to find a massive tumor on the outside of his colon wall. Being where it was located, it had gone undetected with normal checkups and turned into a nightmare of highs and lows.

First, a biopsy showed no cancer-yippee-elation. Next day, bloodwork shows extreme infection that needed to be addressed ASAP. After a week on heavy antibiotics, the surgeon says we need to do exploratory to see what's going on. It turned out the infection was from the tumor that had ruptured and spread. After this first surgery, Roy was wheeled into a room and the nurses took over. I came in to see if he was awake yet. I saw the stem to stern incision and about fainted… I practically yelled, "What did you do to him!" No one had told me that with that much infection, you leave the wound open to drain. I went into the hallway, shocked and so angry at them all, for what they did and for letting me see that type of wound with no warning of what it was going to look like. You can't keep me down for long. I took some deep breaths and marched back in his room and said, "Let me see, and what is the prognosis?" I then went to the head nurse's station and shook my finger in her face and demanded to talk to the surgeon. She immediately got him on the phone; you are entitled to answers!

Roy had a lot of problems with the antibiotics, throwing up and nausea, etc. Being there every day, I knew which sequence worked the best. The nurses would have shift change and I would be right there watching the order in which they dispensed meds. Just because there is a chart, sometimes the nurses get busy and don't read it.

The surgeon recommended radiation and chemo about two weeks after surgery. Roy had not even healed yet; this isn't good. Now this kind of treatment is a personal choice, one I would not have chosen for myself or for him, but it was his decision and I honored his wishes. Chemo three times a week for the rest of his life we were told, in addition to radiation every day for three weeks. I learned when he was sick if it was from the meds and could we handle it, or do I call 911. During this first year, we had our wills and proxies done. The Lord put a wonderful financial planner in our lives. She knew how to secure our 401(k) from his work and get it so we could use it to live. We had to keep insurance intact with no job as he was so sick. It took some doing, but we were able to get disability. We were so busy running for treatments that we did not know how, or to be truthful, even care at that point, but she stepped in and did it all.

This first year after diagnosis, we maintained hope. We had a woodcutting afternoon with family and friends as I had ordered a load of logs and it had to get cut and split before winter. We spent some time at our camp in the woods; we even got a puppy. Then the chemo stopped working. The doctors said he qualified for a new drug that was in trial phase and not approved yet, but conventional drugs for this cancer were not holding it at bay anymore. Roy had his first treatment, but the tumor had grown and now he required another surgery. This necessitated another week stay in the hospital. By the time he came home, he had missed too many treatments and was disqualified from the trial. Now there was no more medical treatments available to us.

Roy had a total of five such surgeries in one and a half years, each time taking more of the colon out and reattaching around the tumor. Most of this time we were sheltering each other by not discussing what was going on; it was not like we needed to say it. Our time together was now limited, and there exists a closeness as a couple you know you can't experience again later.

His last surgery was the proverbial "carrot," a last chance of removing this piece of tissue that was running our lives. A specialist in Rochester thought he could get it; only problem was, Roy needed to be off previous meds for a month prior so there would be no excessive bleeding issues. There is a large display screen, like you see at airports, where it shows the time the patient goes in for surgery, then in to recovery, then into his room. My daughter and I watched it as he went into the OR. Within half an hour, it showed him in recovery; this is not a good sign. The surgeon met with us and said if he took out the tumor, it would kill him as it had attached to other organs. Now hope is gone, but we have each other right now and were not throwing away our remaining moments.

My daughter and I were staying at a hotel in Rochester for the week while he recuperated enough to bring him home. Whether from lack of sleep or from stress overload, everything seemed funny. The doctors had put Roy on meds to help him sleep; that was counterproductive. He was whistling for the dog and building his projects in the air with his hands. My daughter went to the nurses' station and said, "What did you give my father, LSD?" Guess that apple didn't fall far from the tree. The meds weren't harmful but had to wear off. We had them put the bed alarm on so they would hear if he tried to get up. We headed back to the hotel and went to the small cafeteria they had there as we hadn't eaten all day. By this time, we had left exhaustion way behind us and were functioning on adrenalin. The café was still open so we got a table and food and a drink. I was on my cell phone reporting home, and she was doing the same on hers. We started talking louder then looked at each other and said we should be quieter as there were others eating also. Looking around at the other diners, we burst out laughing. I swear I think there was a deaf convention going on as all were using sign language. How bizarre.

Back at the hospital, the nursing staff came in regularly to do vitals, etc., and when they left, we asked them to either shut the door or partially close it to keep activity at a minimum. Several times a nurse would poke her head in and comment on the "peaceful" feeling in the room.

The second year after the cancer diagnosis is hard to describe. This disease had taken us through all kinds of battles. I lost forty pounds and was using safety pins to hold up my pants. I would come home from the hospital totally spent, grab a sandwich and a quick bath, return a few phone calls, and get in bed—repeat again tomorrow and the day after; the entire year, it was spent in a hospital every few weeks. Not only did I try to stay positive for my husband, I had the home front to maintain, keeping bills paid and our kids informed without losing all hope. I don't believe I was in denial or the depths of despair, I was just *alone*. Such an easy word that has such horrible feelings attached. Yes, I have family and friends, but I needed more courage to deal with what lay ahead. When my husband came home from the hospital the final time, we were joyous as he was where he wanted to be. He got as far as the sofa just once and wanted to go back to bed. His energy and will to live was about spent. I knew when he couldn't get out to his shed and work on his projects, that our time left was short.

Roy's hospital bed was in our room in front of my closet, so every time I needed something, I had to go around the bed. Once such morning, I was looking for a shirt when Roy gave me a feeble push into the closet. What a meathead, to be able to do that still was pretty darn good. He got to say all his good-byes right down to the dogs. Now, I have not gone into lengthy detail about anyone's illness as they were all personal experiences, and even though they are no longer here, I respect them as if they were.

This may be hard to read for some of you, but I have experienced circumstances over and over as I watch the end come closer. I have never seen at the actual time of death any person be afraid. Instead I have noticed how the mind protects, by either a coma-like state, or by regressing and seeing long-gone relatives. Of course, in today's modern world, we generally have the help of medication. After witnessing so many depart, for me, it is a continuation of learning at a higher level, spiritual growth, and gaining a better understanding in how to help.

Let me explain the interaction when a soul leaves its human body. I look into unseeing eyes and assure him that it's okay to go; we will be fine here. You have worked too long and too hard and you need to rest. God is calling you home. Jesus, please take this special child of yours into your waiting arms and have mercy and peace for us left behind. I continue looking into his eyes, two short breaths later, and an emptiness fills the room. That is all that is left behind after this huge battle to stay is lost. In the blink of an eye, he is gone and the room is quiet. Peace surrounds us; reality can come later.

I had told my pastor on one of our trips to the hospital that Jesus was not in the heavens; he was walking right by my side, step by step as my friend and savior, and I now know a closeness with him that I had not realized before was possible.

Every ambulance ride, Roy and I did was we, not he.

Every doctor visit, it was also we, not he.

It was always as one that my husband and I approached life and death. Life's' lessons are here every day—protectiveness, true love, empathy, dignity, humor. Whether you believe in a higher being or are an atheist or just don't know, you need a connection to hold on to in times of grief and sadness as much as you do in happier more joyous moments. We look for someone to share this with, but we are never alone in our lives if we turn within.

After Roy died, I had everyone leave the room and closed the door so it was just us. I combed his hair with my fingers, kissed his brow and cheeks, and said good-bye, alone. I then take a deep breath, figuratively and literally. My whole identity of "self" has just changed. I will need everything in my arsenal at hand to truly understand all that has happened. It is not all sorrow and pain, but moments of humor and bonds of closeness. You will experience humility, crushing grief, moments of laughter—so much love that must last the rest of your life. I once told my husband, "I loved you your whole life, I will miss you the rest of mine."

I get up the next morning looking to reinvent myself, no longer a wife or caretaker; my lifelong best friend is gone. To escape the pain, I find myself going to bed very early each night, not that much sleep will come. It will get better I am told, remember the forty years you had. This does not help at all! I hope to catch myself if I ever feel like saying that. It is hurtful, it is meant to help, but it does not. It negates the time we had and now do not. It is not meant unkindly, just not in understanding where I am at this time.

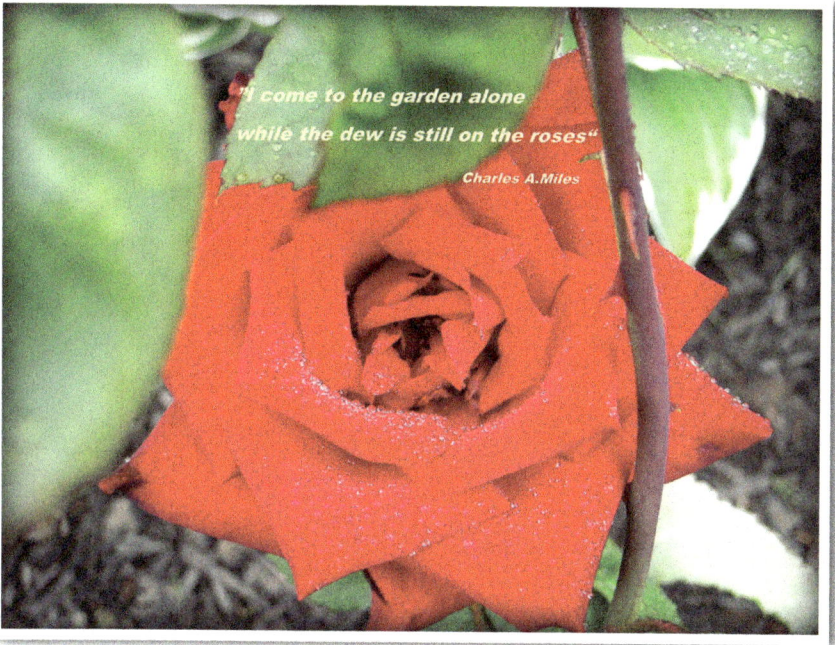

I come to the garden alone, while
The dew is still on the roses
And the voice I hear, falling on
My ear, the Son of God discloses.

And He walks with me, and he talks
With me, and he tells me I am
His own. And the joy we share
As we tarry there, none other, has
Ever known.
—Charles A. Miles

Written to bring hope to the hopeless, rest for the weary,
And downy pillows to dying beds.

Less than a year after Roy's passing, my mother wanted to move in. She had been living independently since Dad had died, and now was eighty years old and getting scared of living alone. Truthfully, I think she was going to take care of me. The day she moved in was a Friday. She got as far as my sofa and lay in a fetal position the entire weekend with severe back pain. Again, as a family, we took her by ambulance to the ER.

She had never been in an ambulance or even a hospital except when she had us kids. Well, we ended up getting a doctor that was not sympathetic to older people, and I am being kind here, what I would like to say is he was brain dead from the neck up. Now this sentence is probably not the Christian thing to say, but there is anger that needs an outlet also during all these "life events." He gave her a quickie exam and said no ribs were broken and gave her a pain pill and sent us home. Now my mom is not one to complain, so if she said something was wrong, you knew it was bad. Second trip to the ER within the week and I told the nurses I wanted a real doctor this time. She said, "All our doctors are real doctors." She had no idea what was coming next. After the two years I had just been through, I was taking no prisoners. I told her, "I beg to differ with you! If that were true, we wouldn't be here twice in one week!" A set of back X-rays were done, how about that, pain in the back shown very clearly in back X-rays instead of chest X-rays. This exam showed seven compound fractures in Mom's back, some healed and some new. This would be why she was in so much pain. She was admitted for pain management. The machines connected to her kept going off as her blood pressure skyrocketed. It took a week to get this pain under control and then we brought her back to my house. The very next day, we headed back by ambulance again. All these heavy-duty pain meds were having effects on her breathing; she had COPD and asthma and the opioids gave her severe constipation. She went in the hospital weighing ninety-four pounds and came home a week later some pounds lighter. The medication for the constipation worked to the extent that she lost a lot of fluid and potassium and became dehydrated. It was at this time we almost lost her. I called 911, and this time, we went to a different hospital. Again, she was admitted with "hospital-acquired pneumonia and UTI." She was distraught to the point of crying and telling me it was enough. She quit eating and refused physical therapy. Can you imagine your mom crying to come home and being too weak to produce tears? My Mommy crying— never, except when my brother died. She said, "I am done." I knew exactly what she meant; she had enough! I told her, "I understand, and I will get you home!"

Without God's help, I probably would have been in the bed with her. So much pain, no let up for her. I thanked God every day for his strength and for my sister, without whom I would have been left alone to handle this new crisis.

We brought her home by medic-van weighing sixty-four pounds and still not able to eat. Now, I can't fix sixty-four pounds! Hospice came but would only do what we asked by way of getting what we needed, i.e. medications, supplies, and contacting the doctors, and when the time came, the funeral director.

Mom had a rough time of letting go. One day would be "I am to tired" to "when I get better." One morning, my sister, having just gotten up, was gathering supplies from Mom's room to take to the kitchen. Mom says, "She looks like a mad scientist, don't tell her," which of course I had to do. It was funny and unexpected. Everyone should have the right to decide when enough is enough. Mom did not want to eat; I told her that was fine. She did not want therapy; once again, I told her that I agreed with her. It was her personal choice to be made with a clear mind. I will honor her wishes. My siblings had a bit more of a problem accepting this situation, but because of all I had been through, I understood where Mom's emotions and physical limits were at this time.

Toward the end, I told her, "Okay, I'm going to get the Big Guns out now!" I went for the Bible and read her the Lord's Prayer and other passages. I am not sure she could hear, but it helped me. When it finally came her time to pass, it was just her and me in the room. My sister had just gone outside to walk the kinks out of her back. I always knew it would be just the two of us. I said, "Mom, I am here holding your hand. Now reach out with your other hand and grab David's and we will never be separated." This is when she left. Once again, two small gasps and the light in her eyes was gone. At peace at last. OMG! I am an orphan and a widow in less than a year!

About a week has passed before I began to realize what I have been through. I had not yet processed Roy's death and now this is dumped on me too. My husband of forever was gone, and it seems a split second later my mom is also gone. I finally break down and fall apart. I am literally shattered and splintered. It was fourteen hours of weeping, sometimes gut-wrenching sobs on my knees, other times just tears rolling down my face with no control. This moment my walk with Jesus became a reality in my life, a part of me, and I guess he was there the whole time. This conclusion I was told by "HIM" to write and share and that it was *very* important. This is the entire reason for this book.

Conclusion

Having literally been on my knees with grief, I turn to God for help in understanding, coping, and even in forgiveness for any transgressions made or not made. Not being able to continue and knowing it should not be a sign of weakness or even human failing, but one of strength in knowing without doubt your God will pick you up and carry you through your personal journey to Him. No other will have your travels to go through—each has their own path in life. It is an extremely personal decision in not only which direction you take, but the fortitude it will take you to do it. You cannot do it alone! Friends will try to comfort, family members see things through their own experiences, but only you and your God can do this together.

There is an end for us all; none of it pleasant, but in saying that, there is without doubt also a beginning. When I can physically see with my own eyes a soul leave its earthly body, it is a miraculous sight that cannot and should not be forgotten as we all have to go thru this process to get to Him. Without this hope, there is no meaning here at all, rather something to get through and grab at the smallest of joys. I can only imagine from all this sorrow that true forgiveness and strength, and most of all, love awaits us; nothing less will do for me. God has heard my cries and has given me peace. By writing this down, I hope others suffering sorrows too much to bear can also be comforted by His hand.

I'm like a dandelion blowing in the wind, on wishes from a child in a quiet voice unheard.

Please, dear Lord, grant me one wish, to never lose the music in all that you have done.

Not to leave any stone upturned, nor the smallest of your lessons unlearned.

When I can no longer hear the music, please bring comfort to those around me.

A larger chorus will be singing, awaiting my return.

Like a murmur in the wind, from a quiet voice unheard.

I am taking a step back for self-preservation, looking (and writing) at the past to see where the future is headed. I need to be careful as I feel as though I have been through a trial by fire.

About the Author

A true nature lover, you will not find this author inside very often, but rather in the woods on hiking trails and taking photos. She is a photographer, along with the keen eye that misses little and sees much. Her love for her family and pets are evident in her photos and her words. Accompanied by her two cocker spaniels, often traipsing over meadows and fields, looking for the unexpected. Having lived her whole life in a small town in Upstate New York, she values the sense of community and bonds of friendship with those she meets.

CPSIA information can be obtained
at www.ICGtesting.com
Printed in the USA
BVOW05s1645080617

486350BV00003B/12/P